D1615979

THE LIGHT STATION ON TILLAMOOK ROCK

ARROWOOD BOOKS
CORVALLIS, OREGON

MADELINE DE FREES

THE LIGHT STATION
ON TILLAMOOK ROCK

Illustrated by ROSALYN RICHARDS

Earlier versions of this poem appeared in *Shenandoah*
and in *The Paris Review*.
This trade edition published by arrangement with
The Press of Appletree Alley.
Printed in the United States of America.
Arrowood Books, Inc., P. O. Box 2100, Corvallis, Oregon 97339.

Library of Congress Cataloging-in-Publication Data
DeFrees, Madeline.
    The light station on Tillamook Rock / Madeline DeFrees;
illustrated by Rosalyn Richards.
        p. cm.

ISBN 0-934847-12-6 (acid free)
    1. Tillamook Rock Light Station—Poetry. 2. Lighthouses—Poetry.
I. Title.
PS3554.E4L54   1990
811'.54-dc20   90-43570
                                                CIP

For H.H., a harbor light, a port in a storm

PREFACE

In 1981, during a year off from teaching, I returned to my native state and leased a house in Cannon Beach, Oregon, overlooking the Pacific Ocean not far from Tillamook Rock. I remained there from August of that year until June 1982. My chief object was to achieve the solitude needed for writing, but also, and more specifically, to spend a winter by the sea, testing whether I might like to retire there when the time came. Although I found the sea's more dramatic moods inspiring, I felt unequal to the demands of permanent residence on that storm-wracked coast.

Even before leaving New England, I had been reading intensively on memory and perception, especially in Julian Jaynes's book, *The Origin of Consciousness in the Breakdown of the Bicameral Mind*. I continued to reflect on these subjects, supplementing my abstract inquiries with others on the physical realities of my new environment: the sea itself, intertidal life, weather and climate, local landmarks.

When I learned that a former lighthouse on an offshore rock had become a columbarium or burial place for ashes of the dead, my curiosity led me in pursuit of the story. James A. Gibbs's book on the building of the light station gave me much of the information I needed, and newspaper files picked up the account from there.

I learned that the name *Tillamook* was taken from a large tribe of Salish Indians living near and south of Tillamook Head. In Lewis and Clark's journals, it appears as

Kilamox and *Killamuck*. The height of Tillamook Head and the need to construct a road disqualified that site for the lighthouse. In its stead, Tillamook Rock was chosen. A mile offshore, the Rock is in seas so rough that a Portland mason, experienced in lighthouse work off England's coast, was drowned in the construction survey in 1879.

In spite of the accident, authorities hired a replacement and work moved forward. A little more than twenty-nine feet was blasted off the pinnacle of the Rock to provide a platform. All materials and supplies were landed by derricks. In 1880, construction was completed. The station was officially closed in 1957, replaced by a radar buoy. The lighthouse and the Rock next went through a series of private owners until 1980 when they were purchased by a Portland real estate consortium for use as a columbarium.

Combining on-the-scene observation with reading gave me rich material for writing, much of it concentrated on this long poem or sequence with its submerged story of Tillamook Lighthouse, intertwined with a more personal narrative. The catalogues of Northwest plants in Section V; of geographic names in XII; and in XVI, of vessels shipwrecked during my year of residence take their form from the Holy Week litanies of the Roman Catholic Liturgy as performed during most of my convent days.

In any work of this length and duration, one reaches the point at which everything feeds into the poem. Like the sea, which fuses the most disparate materials, the imagination learns to make unlikely connections, and the controlling images acquire an incremental force more difficult to achieve in a brief compass. In my reading of the poem, images of light and water evolve as analogues for human consciousness. Although the place and the persona are unapologetically local, my hope is that both will transcend their subjective geography to resonate on wider shores.

* * *

I wish to thank the John Simon Guggenheim Foundation for a Fellowship in Poetry that gave me nine months on the Pacific Coast with time to write. During the following year, when I was making final revisions, I received support from the National Endowment for the Arts. My thanks also to Lex Runciman, James Tate, and Dian Williams for helpful editorial suggestions.

At the Cannon Beach Book Store, Valerie Ryan and John Buckley were prompt and efficient in ordering the books I needed, and the volunteer staff of the Cannon Beach Library were generous with recommending reference works and lending regional materials. Finally, I wish to thank Richard Howard, poetry editor of *Shenandoah*, and Jonathan Galassi of *Paris Review* for publishing earlier versions of the poem—the former, a full text; the latter, the final section as originally written.

I also wish to credit the following authors, without whose help I could not have written the poem:

Alt, David and Donald W. Hyndman. *Roadside Geology of Oregon*. Missoula, Montana: Mountain Press Publishing Co., 1978.

Anderson, Bette Road. *Weather in the West*. Palo Alto: American West Publishing Co. (Great West Series), 1980.

Carson, Rachel. *The Sea Around Us.* New York: Oxford University Press, 1951.

Gibbs, James A. *Tillamook Light: A True Narrative of Oregon's Tillamook Rock Lighthouse.* Portland, Oregon: Binford & Mort, 1979.

Long, James. "Steady Quake Watcher Scans Watery World." The *Oregon Journal*, February 10, 1982, p.8, column 2.

The staff of the *Daily Astorian* also supplied xeroxes of stories in their files, although I cannot cite specific sources.

Madeline DeFrees
October 1988
Seattle, Washington

THE LIGHT STATION ON TILLAMOOK ROCK

I THE GEOLOGIST'S MAP

THREE LAPS farther right, I might have been
Mormon: born on the Idaho line where the valley
drains into Oregon. Two hundred million
years gone by, Ontario was the edge. I lean
towards the coast, the ballast
of an earlier life.

            At four I moved
west from the Snake winding north
to a country sprung from collision. Cut off
from her past, the continent drifted: bedrock
seafloor, ranges sheared on the bias
building a new margin.

                Falling off edges, I
never did crawl. When I walked,
the world an unsteady place: California
shifting towards Alaska. Today's Steady Quake
Watcher from Newport Scans Wobbly World
by James Long. Face of my brother-in-law,
jaw twice as strong. I know these men,
the watchers: they will not
be moved, even by an earthquake.

                    It is to you
I speak. In 5 or 10 million years, Portlanders

can wave, if you're right, to San Francisco
sliding past on its way to Juneau.
Trusting my feet, now that I've found them,
more than anything afloat or on wheels,
I would leave my imprint
on cement, on rock, or in a book
for the watcher of the future.

                        Walking sandy
shore, I admire my Nike herringbone
beside the waffle-stomper tread, the wider
radials of cars advancing towards
reverse conclusions, and the barefoot print
I can't identify as girl or gull.
Not to mention the peculiar
tread, unchained, the ocean leaves, receding
from its bed.

               Features of the earthquake map:
Africa slowly turning left,
the Mediterranean squeezed into a puddle.
Long ago the Himalayas rose in a cosmic
fender-bender. While California
drifts, the geologic fidget of Puget Sound
and Northwest Oregon, caught as we've always
known, in the middle, reminds us how
the region's better part is drawn
eerily quiet.

II POWER FAILURE

WALKING the shore, Augustine hoped to comprehend
the mystery: darkness welling up to fill
a small depression hollowed out of sand. Being
fond of light—and secrets—I understand
the impulse: the will to know, the wish to be
turned back.

        Mind turns back on itself: flood-
waters recede. What came to light
last week swims farther down. Unscientific as
the television sounds, that experienced
beachcomber frightens me. Flotsam we ignore,
he says, will not return until four years
have passed. I carry pen and paper
as others carry mace.

        My retrieval system
isn't working right. Blame it
on weather, heavy skies. When I'm in bed,
a sailboat heeling over
keels above my head. I can't recall the name.
Centuries of obscurity. All that time,
scientists declare:

        The atmosphere forgets
its past every two weeks. East and west,

those are the breaks. Later, when it doesn't
matter, the legend flashes on
the screen: *submarine volcano forms an island.*
Island gives way to water. Experts say
Crater Lake may be losing its clarity.
All the same, I float to meet my past, hoping
the mist will rise.

18

III BUILDING THE LIGHTHOUSE

THE BUILDERS who raise a lighthouse can engineer
a tower to the sun: of the many
colored pictures legend paints, this view is one
Romantics favor. Man, the challenger
of ocean whose siren warning calms the breakers.
And this, another: the small pale figure
clinging to the rock face like a barnacle above
the hammering Pacific. Both pictures
rely on an angle of vision: believable, each in
turn.

Eight thousand cubic feet of rough, black
Clackamas stone, one foot square by a yard thick
and each block joined to the hard next
link by a copper bar; ninety-six thousand bricks
scale the defiant tower: embody the architect's
plan. Here, we invent a ritual stone
to keep alive the clutch of newly scattered bone
the ocean hoards:

JOHN R. TREWAVES, MASTER MASON

*His light shines still off walls of England's
stormy coast.*

Drowned in Construction Survey
off Oregon's Tillamook Rock. Body
never found.

18 September 1879

Requiescat in Pace

Rest in peace. No rest for the wicked, my dead
mother would say. Less for
the curious, I call to the other side. None for
ambition, climbing whatever mountain's *there*,
danger waving the traveler on.
The natives know enough to stay clear. But we
blast away at what the ocean takes
centuries to build, level the Rock to replace it
with technology, crown it with light, a flag.
The Unknown Sailor went down here.

20

IV SOUNDING THE OCEAN

I HAVE invited the sea into my windswept room.
made the ocean my library,
its bays and shelves, dim carrels in the rock.
The winds I hear
speak volumes, storms that wrack the shore:
the ocean giving up, not
giving up its dead.

          I look for them in pools
and estuaries, some cunning
fragment of an eardrum's anchor
the wild surf beats until it looks like shell
I pick up on the beach, honey-
combed by parasitic sponge: I can no longer
tell its origin.

         That old siren song
to the north. Bad weather
rolls across the waves. Cape Flattery to Cape
Disappointment and out 60 miles — the long
configuration of the coast that drives
the crabber and the salmon-fisher's boat
to hull-strewn graves.

         The silence of the deep
sea is a legend water writes

on water when the mind is still and wind
escapes the city streets,
roaming desert flats we populate with stars,
thick as our fancies. Oceanographers
know better: their echo-sounding given back
at shifting levels, reveals a phantom floor:
squid, fish, or small planktonic
shrimp. The layer moves, vertical migrations
keyed to light and dark.

                    Diatoms sift down
like snow: manna for the deep-sea
creatures—tiny shrimp, one claw enlarged
to stun its victim, clacking
the joints of that sea-based weapon.
Nothing is ever wasted in the sea. Ocean is
a good provider: minute
relics of the smaller dead—shells, skeletons,

souvenirs of cycled and recycled matter. That
astonishing red carpet, rolled out
in the diver's memory, its only jewels, sharks'
teeth and the earbones of whales.
Chemical salts, trace metals—iron, cobalt,
nickel, copper, gold.
Drift of volcanic dust and Arctic Ocean ice-
pack. River silt and silica. Fall of meteoric
debris.

Like a tree crashing in unlit forest,
the sea, viewed in another light,
emits no sound. Only its bonds cry out: shoal
and promontory, cliff, island, fissure, reef.
Lacking noisy tenants, barriers
and weather, water seeks its own level, water
holds its peace.

V THE RETURN FROM NEW ENGLAND

COMING BACK, I walk the beach, the offshore
road, ear quickened to the shells
that amplify and fall into a former
litany: clack of Clackamas and Estacada.
Softer syllables of plants
spilling over banks and gullies. O all ye
holy succulents and sages, We beseech thee,
hear us.

       Oregon grape, barley, Scotch broom,
clover, lupine, thimbleberry, laurel,
morning glory, heather, Canterbury bells. All
that is vaguely Latin
trembles in these shoots. I am breathing
the air of an old benediction. Memory
pulls at the Latin roots. O escalonia,
Spanish cousin, flowering hedge,
whose other name is saxifrage, We beseech
thee, hear us.

       In a world of fixed
responses, these are the rain's gift,
salt air celebration. Calla lilies, our name
for Sisters of Providence, as in Divine,
growing wild in Marshfield, later called
Coos Bay.

The Coast Range falls away,
Cascades, the old declared
dead, every mountain top another story: Hood
where I toasted retreat from the crowd.
The dome of Holy Names: still life of a nun
framed in the studio window. Adams,
rounded at the cone, the Northwest ice cream
ad. St. Helen's restless sleeper.

                            O all ye
saintly conifers and creepers, We beseech thee,
hear us.

           On my knees before the fire, the wood
too green, I feed *New Yorker* pages
to the coals and watch
that elegant four-color blaze: Wedgwood-and-
Tanqueray fire, Christian Dior,
smoke of Royal Copenhagen, Glenlivet fire
and *Eau Sauvage*. Why is it the news
glows with such passion as the margins darken,
the words dissolve, and ashes
creep along the edge?

VI BREACHING THE ROCK

PACIFIC, the true misnomer: around the Columbia
Bar, old salts from Singapore
to London and Seattle recognize some namer's
private joke on the unsuspecting.
The Rock falls plumb into those storied combers:
240 feet of ocean pool
the summer whales frequent to rub off barnacles
against basalt. They dive, cavort, spout freely
without concussion.

          Old-timers took the mission
with more than a grain of salt.
They'd seen their cronies drowned in harebrained
schemes to tame the Rock. This expert,
hired and fired-up by the government, this crazy
builder, Charles Ballantyne,
was predictable hearts-and-flowers. Fishermen
knew the wiles of Terrible Tilly, let him learn
on his own.

          Discouraged, the builder fanned out
over the countryside to sign
eight stone men, innocent of town gossip. Found
the right place to keep them
willing. Seasonal gales had set in early. Talk
was cheap as a beer in every saloon.

Across the river, Cape Disappointment loomed,
the keeper absent, and the skeleton
crew rehearsed in reticence.

                            Twenty-six days of
Disappointment — checkers, whodunit's
and chess — the quarrymen cheered for the revenue
cutter, danger better than this.
Near the Rock, the sea saw their mistake: waves
rampaging, ship astride, cutter
moored to planted buoy, small boat over the side
where Ocean turned to Buffalo Express
stampeding into *Killamuck* Station, into a narrow
cleft.

    Six hours nearer dark they'd landed four
and terrified the others, mainly one
Gruber, 300 pounds or 21 stone of quivering fat,
too big for his breeches buoy. The hoodoo
light guttered ahead. Wiser Indians' celebrated
Land of Many Waters, most of them dangerous,
railroaded the frightened masons back to the old
Disappointment, ready for chess and survival,
ready to settle for less.

VII SCENES OUT OF SEQUENCE: WHAT THE COASTWISE KNOW

THE OLD Coast Guardsman walks along the Seaside
Promenade, mourning the light he tended
two decades of its 77 years. A visitor might
think, How picturesque! That stubborn chunk
of rock, a mile off Tillamook Head:
white-painted stone, black tower
pitched above calm seas.

                      A closer look would
show such treachery, it swells a book
with tales better left untold. Yet the fateful
stand—romantic, doomed—looking out
to sea. I take my stand with them, follow
my history wherever it leads. Ask the locals
who saw their fishermen put a dory in
south of Haystack Rock

                        to take the seasick
private owner to his latest piece
of real estate. Ask the outboard motor crew:
the owner and two others
rescued as they swam, treated for shock. Ask
the fourth who didn't come back
alive. Water takes longer than fire to ready
the body for viewing.

Don't invent a necklace
of anemones, starfish worn like a badge
or barrette. Widows and cosmeticians have been
known to faint, regarding three days'
changes. Water-logged, we say, speaking of
boats and floating timber, not unlike
the swollen bulbs of kelp: shape of an amber
beet tossed up by the tide.

VIII THE UNDERWATER JOURNEY

RED: the first to go. At 300 feet, one waves
good-bye to every orange and yellow
ray of sun. Next, my favorite green fades out.
One thousand feet: pure indigo
remains—deep, brilliant, dark—most living
forms, transparent. The glassy fish swim past,
their ghostly bodies

                    shot through with ocean.
In the clearest water, violet survives another
thousand feet. Then, black.
As if to compensate for that too-early mourning,
prawns wear secret shades: red,
purple, scarlet—yet appear
habited in black. A higher light will show
the true colors.

            "There is a rock awash inside
Tillamook Rock," an eminent observer
writes, and I agree. More
stubborn than the famous pebble of Demosthenes,
that Rock intrudes its pellet in the skull,
a floating weight no probe eliminates before
the breakdown.

I had a friend, address unknown,
whose ID reads: *Cremation* —
ashes thrown into the sea. The wish seems
harmless—one the wind might honor
gladly, without a distribution fee. In any case,
the question's moot. The light
went out. False prophets
claimed the Rock, my life grew dim.

IX THE COLUMBARIUM:
EVERLASTING CONSIDERATION

HOW SHALL we market death? Not that loved one,
faithful dog-at-heel, not the bird-in-hand
worth two, the boa close as a collar,
not the son we married off, the husband
underground before he makes it to the top. We
market the only real—the Self
ensconced in the dome's dark lantern. We tell
our client, Frankly, there is no caretaker
like the cold, considered sea.

                             No visitors who
can't afford the chartered helicopter, no heirs
greedy for sterling and china, no survivors
gloating. Absolute satisfaction
or your money back. No vandals, ritual grave
robbers, no hard-up medical students, artists-
in-anatomy. You owe it to yourself:
your ashes perfectly safe. Eternity-at-Sea:
How beautiful! Starts at six-ninety. Urns
encased in plexiglass. The dead

                           secure beyond
belief. Fees will rise: one to three-thousand
next year. Buy now, move in
later. Only 467 thousand slots. If you're not
a dead star and would like to be

considered for the best spot of all, a founding
member, call today. The Hollywood Hall of Fame
and 25 grand on the line
bring a niche in the lantern room. Eternity at
sea. How many pearl divers,

                                      air travelers, dory
fishermen, mutineers, suicides,
sad captains and cruising wives, no longer soft
to the touch, have made it there for less.

X DEVELOPMENTS

ROMANCE dies harder than ownership, the pleasure
boat anchored off the coast of vision.
No sooner was Tillamook Rock listed in the day's
Real Estate than bold tycoons
were building summer homes high above the storms
for entertaining friends. To own
the island—later, perhaps, a chain! They might
get to know themselves:

                        a new telephone safari,
consulting architects, navigational
maps. They saw themselves training sea anemones
on trellises to keep their mouths
shut, barking sea lions in hoops to open up and
speak. The maid would serve
hors d'oeuvres to the Tufted Puffins every other
week: stuffed squid, shad, poached
lobster and crab.

                They'd name fictitious beasts
and fence a patch of wild between tennis
and croquet. All the way to Venice, California,
their bright plots flickered
through the news and came to grief on real waves
real rock. Lights of far-off summer
homes went down in baubles: a ship in a bottle,
their will to stay alive.

36

XI QUESTIONS OF OWNERSHIP

AT 25, the well-groomed bachelor invests in Coca
Cola souvenirs. He allows it would not
be inaccurate to call him
rich. He smiles for the camera. His interests
lately grown to take in the retired
lighthouse, he's known by almost everyone
inspired to love the limelight best.

                    The old
Disappointment lens. The private and the public
face. Landscapes repeated through a glass
darkly as the radio
cautions against optimism and the media never
quit. Hymns to extinguished light we counted on
to guide us to the right channel, keep us
safe from shipwreck.

              He sold out—was selling
out, even as he told reporters
he wouldn't let the Rock change hands for
under a million. So much for grandstand
acrobatics. Listed in L. A. for 750 thousand,
the lighthouse was a giveaway in the end.

He settled out of court with a woman of 74 who
called him a swindler. Gave her

the Rock, long since reclaimed by cormorants
and grebes. The biggest guano factory
yet discovered in the free
world, the doryman had said, that day the new
owner in sport coat and tie
lost the first bout with *mal de mer*.

XII GEOGRAPHY AS WARNING

THE WILDCAT drilling started in 1919, the year
of my birth. The legend grows. Where
then, was Lion Rock, two feet
offshore, the mane a halo and the claws
retracted as if something more could be expected
of the sleeping form
the ocean gives a voice? An active coastline —
land, risen; or sea level, dropped: swales,
breaker bars and scarps. The fracture
zones. At the bottom of a bay
lies the Millicoma floodplain, Morphic river-
tongues in thousands, whose meaning
no one knows.

        The Seaside Nat, *circa* 1928.
In the heated pool I stroked away ocean shock,
my heart developing a slight
murmur. Even then Pacific waters meant a mutual
embrace. Rockaway at 10, starfish
clinging to the rocks we balanced on. Black gym
bloomers, sailor blouse, knit beret: I
am the younger version of those boaters, argyles
and golf knickers: women in short
skirts and slingback shoes, there on the putting
green.

        Later, Agate Beach, white-ribbon stone
cut and polished for my first ring.
Newport and rhododendron. Bandon in April, wind
an evil force. Abandoned by a traveling
superior who planned this Arctic curse, an early
spring picnic, we shivered
by a three-foot wall until, at five, our driver
back, we were delivered
to our winter home.

                Gearhart, our isolated
summer place. Old nuns and sickly younger ones
kept busy those strong enough to work.
Mid-forties, then, we sneaked in twenties bathing
suits, out the back door, over the hill,

to reappear as tourists, believing they couldn't
tell. Medieval costumes, a giveaway,
not to mention white arms and whiter legs.
Limbs, an old nun called them. "I'd like a
limb of lamb," on Saturday.

                  Next, Lincoln City:
holiday on the fringe. Writing up a storm
through that perfect week, the disk
mending slowly. Years after, balanced between
out and in, and ready for the perfect
ending, a trip to Neah Bay, I saw our friend,
Skipper, slam the car door on his index
finger and sweated out the day. The old wounds
open like anemones. We
pray them shut.

           The names float like buoys of
every kind—lighted whistle, spar
buoy, can, nun buoy, bell, and we are on our
knees again, map spread out like comics:

                      Cape
Sebastian where the arrows fell. O all ye canny
mariners and martyrs, Pray for us. O
all ye terrors lurking off the coast, Pray
for us. O all ye inland patrons of the lost,
Ora pro nobis.

Cape Lookout mapped as a dagger,
Pray for us. Cape Perpetua
gored by wild beasts, Pray for us. Cape Shoal-
water, Cape Foulweather, Destruction
Island, Camp Castaway, Spare us
O Lord.

Cannibal Mountain, Butcherknife Creek,
Turnagain Arm, Quicksand Bay, Devil's
Churn, Spouting Horn, Boiler Bay, Turn not away
Your Face from us, Hear us, O Lord,
Have Mercy.

The oceanic floor: anatomy becomes
familiar as the forms we walk inside.
Wrecks containing treasure, the flowering skull.

XIII MICROCLIMATES

WHEREVER a wall rises to keep off wind, where
trees are planted to provide
the shade we need in summer, a small sanctuary
waits. We know these territorial
rights: refuge for seagoing
wings, Seal Harbor, sea lions' disputed Rock.
A room of one's own in mid-ocean,
alive or dead—a cold shock we learn to call a
challenge.

No moat surrounds my coastal home,
and yet the rain creates one.
I keep the drawbridge raised against the Bible
salesmen, shut venetian blinds.
The welcome mat's a one-way read: welcomes me
leaving the house. In humid weather,
artichokes and pine cones
close in on themselves.

A lizard on a rock
slab in the sun defines his own
passive solar system. My front door's hidden
on the side, the street face
blank as a mausoleum. Caves invent their own
worlds, devoid of seasons. A dry

cave may survive thousands of years. Wet caves,
grown old, collapse, surprised
by running water.

XIV STORM WARNINGS

THE SKINS of onions thicken underground, build
their nested walls to guard the white
center: layer on layer rounding
outward to the yellow husk. It will be a hard
winter. In the corral, dusky horses
tense their necks and sniff the air. Field
mice scurry in and out of holes.
In John Day country, sheep huddle by the fence.
A storm is on its way.

             Like school children
waiting for a bus, young haddock take
shelter under the great bell
of a jellyfish, trailing long tentacles, travel
the sea in tandem. If we revel in the random
fall of consequential rain, we let
these drops collect, disperse, on cove & inlet.
The elements transposed and fused,
transfused and posed in the mind's eye, beside
themselves: satellites of water particles
orbit the forms of waves.

             See how the ocean
handles waste: glass released of its edge
in the hurl and clash of tide.
Light follows a windy mazurka on the surface

46

of the shallows. Small wonder fish discover
few landmarks in the sea. Where
geology and weather intersect, imagine me
walking the shore. My shoes
fill with water. I move to driftwood
fires of early summers, back in time, deeper
towards that old down-bending ocean floor.

Up here, a sea opaque as witches' brew — cold
as Potomac ice, guarding its dead.
World is a real place, illusionary
always. Farther out, beyond the sand and mud,
those microscopic one-celled
animals, *radiolaria*: riddled silica of matter
shared with quartz and sandy beach,
with semi-precious stone. Fire-opal of my ring
reminds me: Carefully tended, even the greenest
heartwood glows, though what it does
to the chimney is another
chapter, and to the kindling, darker still.

XV THE FIRST LANDING

WHERE there's much light, shadows are deepest,
Goethe said. Over the portal of the river
mouth, on the other side, the unlit
tower of Cape Disappointment waited two years.
Light came at last through perfect
French prisms. The oil that lantern burned
was legendary. Men lugged
their burden up the stair—170 gallons monthly,
to the hungry monster.

                  There, beyond Astoria
and its clacking tongues, in the forsaken
keeper's house, Ballantyne hid his crew 26 days
until their tempers shortened
and the seas grew calm. Not calm enough, as it
happened. October 21, 1879, half the men
made a landing on that wild Rock
before the angry ocean turned the others back.

October 21 was Founder's Day at old St. Mary's,
Portland. We took our boarders'
lunch from planks, laid across two barrels,
a re-enactment of the nuns'
first days in the Lounsdale House 20 years
before the Rock landing. On the second floor,
the sanctuary lamp glowed red,

a candle always lighted in the chapel where I
prayed to join them

              and after that, for holy
perseverance. In writing, I reversed north-
flowing rivers remembering
the future, *déja vu.*

XVI COUNTING THE WINTER DEAD

OFF the Oregon coast, 33 in storm and sudden
squall. Fifteen boats gone down.
Where do they lead: risks the gill-netters take
gambling hard lives against the waves,
skill against the tide? If hands on the tiller
shake, let Valéry sing
their ashes to rest in vaults of Tillamook Light
turned Columbary-by-the-Sea.

                           Turn back, sad
fisherman, we might have said, before the last
wave finds you with your
proud back turned. The ocean knocked at cabin
windows. Water followed you inside
your second skin. You were alone, we know.
The rest is guesswork and a corpse
washed in. The suit you called survival
made a shroud.

The Mary Jean, Inez, the Merrimac, the Oregon
Otter. Spare us, O Lord!
O all ye vessels, plying wild water, Spare us!
O all ye fishers of the deep:
The Annie B, the Frank, the Sean, Christina J,
Mariah and Aloha, the myth-making Cygnet.

O every underwater magnet,
drawing to our doom, Parce nobis, Domine!

The Debonair, Sagacious, the Odyssey, Avenger,
We beseech thee for a sign! Rangers
off the headlands. O all ye
watchers of the sky and scanners of the wave!
O every creature,
voracious and benign, Spare us O Lord!

XVII THE BOOK OF SEDIMENTS

EYE is an ocean bounded on every side by desert,
the salt shore framing the wide
salt sea. Mourning on land, mine's the drooping
habit of weeping willow. Mid-Pacific
tears are rain, stunning the oysters open: seed
the ancients held
responsible for pearls. On my nightstand

lamplight glows, a glass base filled with shells
containing news of ocean. If the shell encloses
what the sea says to the listener,
every whorl and coil reveals the secrets there.
Down the long evolutionary avenues, some random
turning called the Veiled
Pacific Chiton and knew the walled slow way

the embryo, even then, was tending. Chiton-like,
an armadillo of the sea,
I grew a shell before I went to school.
Though water is my element I cannot relax in it:
where is he now—father, messiah, lifeguard,
unburnished lover and friend—who, more than any
other, believed in the lost
free-swimming self?

Waterborne among the Common
Scorpio Conchs, I search the hard way
back. Attached to wharves and rocks I recognize
the blue mussels and cling to the sources
of a truer life. The sea is a source. Consider
the subterfuges of the sea: the scallop's
myriad eyes, poison of cones, dark dye of squid,
anchor thread and cuttlebone.

Given the choice
between toothpaste and ink, I know
where my loyalties lie. The rarer False Scorpio
Conch, for a while believed not to exist,
acknowledged at last: my reminder of everything
flawed. In the imperfect tropics,
venom matches paradise: not even heaven secure.
If I called you now

unsure over darkening waters
would you hear me? In the shy littoral
snail, I follow the clockwise coiling of shells,
admiring clumsy clams and sedentary
oysters. You imagined yourself at night tossing
your tired body, the unsteady heart
in your chest, over the riverbank into flotillas
of sleep.

At midnight, startled awake, I see my
self adrift on the vast dark,
the raft Kon-tiki, the night lights on: the pale

moon jelly Aurelia swaying the chains
of a bright arcade, going where wind and waves
take me. Balsa logs,
bamboo hut, my frail shelter, the exact analogue
for the universal voyage.

The darker the night,
the more life pressed around us. Bold survivors
embroider a theme of hunger and pursuit,
the phosphorescent, bug-eyed creatures rising up
from the unknown deep. Shadowy
gulls hover over silver-sided fish flashing past
to safer waters, disappear
in the predatory swoop as though sparks of Roman
candles.

Ship Harbor Inn—high above the Sound,
we slept while frogs and crickets made
a fluttering circle on the ear's horizon. Heard
one long note, the foghorn cutting
in and out of sleep. Like waves we know our ore
by weight. Neatly we sort out beds of separate
deposits: gold from monazite, red
garnet from zircon. Disaster always in our wake,
we stumble on, sifting platinum

from chromite,
grain by grain. Some regard the ocean prospect,
make themselves minor prophets; others have gone

for broke. Isn't that Gruber there,
the 300-pound quarryman we left, too fat
to fit in, refusing to be tied? His mid-section
circled by two life preservers, he made it over,
the first to pass dry-shod.

                            Sun-drenched sepals
in the old stereoscope: two complementary views
(right eye and left) on film the brain
registers and light fuses to a third dimension.
In this one, the ferry's docking at Shaw Island:
a brown-robed nun in pill-box hat
with veil attached, runs down
the gangplank. Clank of heavy chains, and then,
double dissolve into Friday

                            Harbor Whale Museum,
where we saw a brain three times our size.
Remember the days we took to let the sea settle?
Bald Hill and Dinner Island? Cape San Juan
and Sunset Point. I tried the public
telephone: a killer whale was on the line. Off
the hook, a foreign body, flailing, broke
through undreamed light and water.

BIOGRAPHY

Madeline DeFrees began writing *The Light Station on Tillamook Rock* during a nine month residency in Cannon Beach, Oregon. Born in Ontario, Oregon, she has spent most of her life in the Pacific Northwest and currently lives in Seattle, Washington.

She received a B.A. from Marylhurst College and an M.A. from the University of Oregon. From 1936 until 1974 she was a Sister of the Holy Names of Jesus and Mary, and she published her first book of poems, *From the Darkroom* (1964), under the name Sister Mary Gilbert. She taught at a number of colleges and universities, including Holy Names College (Spokane, Washington), the University of Montana, and the University of Massachusetts at Amherst, where she directed a Master of Fine Arts program in creative writing.

DeFrees is the author of five books as well as a chapbook. Her short fiction has been featured in Martha Foley's *Best American Short Stories*. Her other poetry collections include *When Sky Lets Go* (1978) and *Magpie on the Gallows* (1982). Her work has been honored by grants from the National Endowment for the Arts and from the Guggenheim Foundation.

This trade edition of *The Light Station on Tillamook Rock* is reproduced from the limited edition of 150 copies printed and published by The Press of Appletree Alley, which was hand-set by Juanita Bishop in Van Dijck type and designed and printed by Barnard Taylor. The woodcuts are by Rosalyn Richards. This book is printed on acid free paper.